THE TRUE STORY OF CHRISTMAS

Written and Illustrated by Scott Freeman
in Fidelity to the Judeo–Christian Scriptures

BIG PICTURE PUBLISHING
Loveland, Colorado

Mail requests to:
Permissions, Big Picture Publishing, 185 Harrison Avenue, Loveland, CO 80537
email: books@bigpicturepublishing.com

Special thanks to John Meyer, Pat Sokoll, Jonathan Williams, and Kristin Fenwick

Library of Congress Catalogue-in-Publication-Data
Freeman, Scott. The True Story of Christmas / by Scott Freeman; illustrated by Scott Freeman
p.   cm.   Summary: Retraces the biblical story of creation, the fall of man, the creation of Israel,
and God's fulfillment of his plan to fix his broken world by sending a savior for all of humanity.

Printed in the United States of America

ISBN 978-0-9906097-9-7

Dedicated to
Caleb, Lee, Sierra, Joel, and Renee,
who fill my life with love and joy.

And God saw everything that He had made,
and behold, it was very good.

The true story of Christmas begins
at the very beginning, when God created the world.
God is good, and everything He made was good.
In the beginning the whole world was filled with
God's goodness and light.

There was no evil in the world - no fighting,
no sickness, no sadness, no cruelty, no hatred,
no lying, and no death. Above all the rest of
creation, God made human beings to be special
- to be like Him. God gave the first family,
Adam and Eve, a special job to take care of His
good world. We were all made to be God's
sons and daughters, and to be God's friends.

Then, something terrible happened.
Adam and Eve decided to disobey God.

This broke apart the perfect unity they had with God,
with each other, and with God's good world.
After this, God's Spirit and life no longer filled them.
Evil and death entered God's world and changed it
for everyone. Adam and Eve had children, and these
children were also born without God's light.
We are all children of Adam and Eve.

The story of Christmas is about how God still loves us.
Christmas is about His good plan to create a way for us
to receive His love, light, and life again.

After death entered the world through Adam, people became very bad. They hurt each other every day. God decided to destroy the world with a flood, and start over with a man named Noah and his family. After the flood was over, God began His plan to fix His broken world.

He chose Abraham, a man who believed in Him.
Abraham trusted God. God promised Abraham that
a great nation would come from him. This nation
would be a blessing to the whole world.
This nation came to be known as Israel.

God made Israel to be His own people, and their role
was to be a light to the world and to point all people
in the world to the one, true God. Sometimes Israel
did this very well. Sometimes they did not.

But there is one thing that Israel gave to the world
that is more important than anything else.
Through His people, Israel, God sent into the world
a very special child who would bring God's light
back into the whole world.

A brave and faithful shepherd boy named David became Israel's greatest King. God promised David that the special child would come from his family one day.

Long ago in Israel, God would sometimes choose
certain people to be his messegers. These people
were called prophets. They would speak the truth
about God to everyone. Sometimes they would tell
of promises from God that would not come true for
hundreds of years, and Israel would have to wait.

Many of the prophets told of the child who would come;
a child who would bring peace, and set up a good kingdom
that would never end. So Israel waited for this child,
whom they would call the Messiah.

The very last prophet to speak of the promised Messiah was named Malachi. After Malachi, there were no more prophets at all in the land of Israel until it was time for the Messiah to be born. Israel had to wait 400 years after Malachi for God's promise to come true.
That is a very long time!

But then, it finally happened!...

Do not be afraid, Mary, for you have found favor with God. And behold, you will conceive in your womb & bear a son, and you shall call his name Jesus. He will be great and will be called the Son of the Most High. And the Lord God will give him the throne of his father David, and of his kingdom there will be no end.

God sent an angel messenger
to a young girl in Israel named Mary.
The angel told Mary not to be afraid
because God was pleased with her.
God was going to give her a baby boy
who would grow up to be very great.
He would be called the Son of God.
He would rule over Israel,
and His kingdom would last forever.
This baby would be given a name
that means "God Saves."
His name would be Jesus.

The long, long wait was finally over.
Mary's baby would be the special child
that everyone had been waiting for!

Mary was promised to be married to a man named Joseph, but baby Jesus was already growing inside of her, just as the angel had said. Joseph was a faithful man. He believed the angel's message, that Mary's baby was from God.

Before the baby was born, Joseph and Mary had to travel to the city of David, which is called Bethlehem. When they arrived it was time for the baby to be born, but the little town of Bethlehem was very crowded with other travelers. There was no room for Mary and Joseph in the guest room, and the only place for them to stay was a room where some animals were kept.

Baby Jesus, the One who would grow up to be
the greatest of all, was born in a poor place, surrounded
by animals, and laid in a manger for a bed. Even though
everyone in Israel was waiting for the Messiah, almost
no one in Israel knew that the long-awaited Messiah
had finally been born!

Jesus, the perfect Son of God and King of all kings,
was not born in a king's palace. He had no soldiers
protecting Him. His mother and earthly father were not
powerful royal rulers. The priests and religious leaders
in Israel did not know about His birth.

Instead, the Messiah entered the world humbly
and quietly, in a way that no one expected.

After the angels left them, the shepherds went to Bethlehem and
found baby Jesus, just as the angel had said. They excitedly told
Mary and Joseph and the people in Bethlehem about the angels

and what they had said about the child. Everyone must have
wondered what would become of this new baby!

When Jesus was still a very small child, another amazing thing happened. Some wise men from a far-away country arrived in Jerusalem, the capital city of Israel. These wise men said they were looking for the child who had been born King of the Jews so that they could worship him! They said they had seen his star in the sky! Everyone in Jerusalem was surprised and troubled by this - even old King Herod.

First, King Herod met with the Jewish priests and learned that the prophets had written that the Messiah would be born in Bethlehem. Next, he secretly met with the wise men and sent them to Bethlehem to find Jesus. Then he told them a terrible lie. He told the wise men to come back and tell him where Jesus lived so that he could go and worship Jesus too.

But really, King Herod wanted to kill Jesus.

The innocent wise men joyfully went to Bethlehem and found
the house where Jesus lived. They bowed down and worshipped him,
and gave him gifts of gold, frankincense, and myrrh.
When it was time for them to go home, they went back to their own
country without telling King Herod where Jesus was because
God warned them about Herod in a dream.

The visit of the wise men was one of the first signs that Jesus
was sent to be the Savior of the whole world, not just for Israel.

After the wise men left Israel, King Herod became very angry.
An angel appeared to Joseph in a dream and told him to quickly take
his family to another country so that Herod could not hurt the child.
So the special family of Jesus secretly left for the land of Egypt.

After King Herod died, Joseph, Mary, and Jesus came back to
the land of Israel. The child, Jesus, grew up there and obeyed His
Father in heaven perfectly.

Jesus showed us how to live, by helping, healing, and loving people.

He taught us about the kingdom of God, and what it would be like.

He taught us how we can be in His kingdom forever.

He loved us so much that He even let Himself die on a cross, so that our sins could be forgiven.

He overpowered death for us by coming back to life, so that we could also have new life with Him.

He gave us the gift of the Holy Spirit to live in our hearts, so we could have hearts that love and follow Him.

He invited us to be His followers, to love and care for one another, to share His good news, and to be a part of His church of light in a world that is still dark.

This is how Jesus brought light and life back into His world. This is how He made the way for each of us to be children and friends of God again.

This is the most important story in the world, and it is what Christmas is all about.

"I am the light of the world.
Whoever follows me will not walk in darkness,
but will have the light of life."
John 8:12

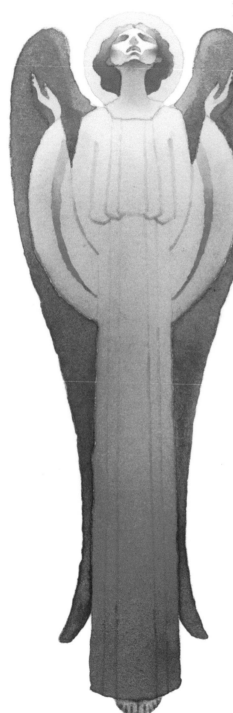

Now you know the meaning of this Christmas carol:

Joy to the world, the Lord is come!
Let earth receive her King;
Let every heart prepare Him room,
And heaven and nature sing,
And heaven and nature sing,
And heaven, and heaven, and nature sing.

No more let sins and sorrows grow,
Nor thorns infest the ground;
He comes to make His blessings flow
Far as the curse is found,
Far as the curse is found,
Far as, far as, the curse is found!

He rules the world with truth and grace,
And makes the nations prove
The glories of His righteousness,
And wonders of His love,
And wonders of His love,
And wonders, wonders of His love.

CPSIA information can be obtained
at www.ICGtesting.com
Printed in the USA
LVHW070924231220
674222LV00011BB/25